*This aerial view looks northward to show the Lone Oak tree (with a picnic table behind it) in the foreground. The Lone Oak trail rises from the bottom of the photo, bends around the tree, and climbs into the hills alongside Vamonos Canyon. Photo by Christa Stoll.*

In the far northeast corner of the Preserve, Radio Tower Road leads to the Five Cities Overlook, a high-elevation hilltop that offers magnificent 360-degree views of the coast and mountains.

Attached to one of the two picnic tables at the site is a notebook that asks, "What legacy do you want to leave in this world?" Inspired visitors who have made it to this glorious spot have answered by filling the pages with joyous messages. A sampling of those messages appears on this page and on page 48.

## "THE BEAUTY OF THE WORLD IS BEFORE YOU."

"Recuerda, como la tortuga, paso a pasito, pero siempre adelante" (Remember, like the turtle, step by step, but always forward).

"Even though life is tough, you need to overcome the hills."

"Beautiful nature for future generations—spread kindness and good will, hike often!"

"Hiked up all the trails up here many times but just found this secluded site today! Glad I did—great spot."

"Epic mountain bike ride to this spot with all the views!"

"Sunshine all the time makes a desert, but let it rain and know the flowers will bloom. Be happy, smile, be healthy, and climb the mountain with your friends! It will be so worth it when you are 80 years old and looking back."

"Happy Mother's Day to all mothers, would-be mothers, Mother Earth, and Divine Mother who gives us love, sunshine, moonlight, stars, flowers, greenery, fruits, vegetables, and life."

"Life is balance. Find something in your life that gives you purpose ... and you will find happiness."

"Be kind, be nice, be joyful."

"Love, and raise children who do the same."

"Life should be lived to the fullest for an entire lifespan. Keep enjoying it until the day you die."

"What a view! If you can't be inspired here, you can't be inspired."

# THE OFFICIAL FIELD GUIDE TO THE PISMO PRESERVE

**Exploring the Wonders of a Central Coast Landmark**

By Chris Strodder and The Land Conservancy of San Luis Obispo County

*A double fly-by over Radio Tower Road.*

**THE OFFICIAL FIELD GUIDE TO THE PISMO PRESERVE**
**Exploring the Wonders of a Central Coast Landmark**

©2025 Chris Strodder and The Land Conservancy of San Luis Obispo County.

All rights reserved. All text and photos by Chris Strodder, except where noted. No portion of this publication may be reproduced, stored, and/or copied electronically (except for academic use as a source), nor transmitted in any form or by any means without the prior written permission of the publisher and/or authors.

Library of Congress Registration: TXu 2-444-569

Name: Strodder, Chris and The Land Conservancy of
San Luis Obispo County (co-authors)
Title: The Official Field Guide to the Pismo Preserve
Publisher: The Land Conservancy of San Luis Obispo County
1137 Pacific Street, San Luis Obispo, CA 93401
www.lcslo.org
Printed in the United States.
Book layout by Pamela Lee, www.pamelalee.me
Trail maps provided by Kyle Walsh and Kendall Gilstrap.
ISBN: 979-8-218-61222-1

*An August view of the Connector mini-trail where it bends towards the south and an ocean view.*

## TABLE OF CONTENTS

Welcome to the Pismo Preserve ... Page vi
History of the Pismo Preserve ... 1
Location and Operations ... 4
Rules ... 6
Animals and Birds at the Pismo Preserve ... 8
A Bouquet of Flowers at the Pismo Preserve ... 10
Exploring the Trails ... 12
Trail Superlatives ... 36
Seasonal Variations ... 38
Recommendations and Etiquette ... 40
About The Land Conservancy ... 44
About the Author ... 46
Pismo Preserve Checklist ... 49

*Observant visitors will often see reminders, like the one shown at left along the Spring to Spring trail on a July morning, of the wildlife that really owns the Pismo Preserve.*

# WELCOME TO THE PISMO PRESERVE

By Kaila Dettman, Executive Director, The Land Conservancy of San Luis Obispo County

"Pismo Preserve–adventure is waiting." In 2014 The Land Conservancy used this slogan to inspire people to support the project and bring the Pismo Preserve to fruition. And while it now has a different meaning, it has never been more accurate than it is today.

The Preserve has something for everyone. This special place welcomes visitors and neighbors alike to explore its rolling hills, breathe in the fresh ocean air, revel in the beautiful views in every direction, and be delighted by the little flowers and critters to be discovered around each bend in the trail. It is a magical place that changes with the seasons, and every day brings a different experience.

Sitting at the top of any of its hills, you can imagine what it would have been like to live here thousands of years ago. Looking out at the humpbacks breaching through the swell in the sea below, you feel more connected to nature and in tune with its rhythms. Walking beneath the canopy of strong and gnarled oak trees, dappled light on the ground below, you can feel at peace and leave the intensity of the rest of the world behind, even if just for a little bit. In the winter little streams flow down the canyons, and the hills come to life, supporting an abundance of both common and rare plants and animals throughout the year–and you realize the Preserve offers so much more than simply a place to recreate.

This property is not just a plot of land and did not happen by chance. Our community came together to protect this place for everyone. It was a herculean effort driven by the recognition that it will benefit generations to come. And our work is not done. In the years ahead the Preserve will rely on people to continue to care for it–ensuring the wild animals can still call it home, and the trails remain fun and accessible for all.

So, I welcome you to dive right in, savor the beauty of the Pismo Preserve, and use this thoughtful book as a guide for your adventures. You won't regret it, and you just might discover something new each time you visit.

Happy trails,

Kaila Dettman, info@lcslo.org

# THE HISTORY OF THE PISMO PRESERVE

*The entrance at 80 Mattie Road, Pismo Beach.*

The Pismo Preserve is the ancestral homeland of yak tityu tityu yak tiłhini Northern Chumash Tribe of San Luis Obispo County and Region (ytt Tribe).

For more than 10,000 years the Central Coast, from what is now San Luis Obispo County to Ventura County, was inhabited by the indigenous Chumash people. With the arrival of Europeans, many Chumash were forcibly removed from their lands without agreement, consideration or compensation.

*Cattle might still be seen at the Preserve, like this contented grazer encountered along the Lone Oak trail early one July morning. In addition to enriching the soil, cattle help reduce the risk of wildland fire by feeding on mustard and grass.*

In 1840, ten years before California became a state, the rolling hills above Pismo Beach became a part of a 9,000-acre land grant given by the acting Mexican governor to descendants of the area's first Spanish colonizers. Parts of this grant, called Rancho Pismo at the time, were sold off to private ranchers. For decades their cattle grazed on the grassy hills among thick oak groves and dense chaparral.

By the twenty-first century, a significant chunk of this land was in the hands of developers who targeted the hills for ambitious new ventures. Just as a row of hotels was ready to rise on Mattie Road along the east side of Highway 101, and with about 16 luxury homes set to be built across the hills, the economic recession of 2008 intervened, slamming the brakes on nascent construction projects.

# THE HISTORY OF THE PISMO PRESERVE

*Carving trails at the embryonic Preserve in 2016. Photos courtesy of LCSLO.*

Rather than continue to pursue commercial and residential development, the owners decided to offer the parcel to The Land Conservancy of San Luis Obispo County (LCSLO). LCSLO, a 501(c)3 nonprofit organization that had already preserved thousands of vulnerable acres throughout the county, eagerly purchased 880 pristine acres for $12.5 million in 2014.

With the agreement in place and the deadline to raise funds looming, Executive Director Kaila Dettman and Deputy Director Daniel Bohlman led a whirlwind effort to unite a consortium of agencies and donors. Money for the newly named Pismo Preserve came from three areas: approximately 65% was contributed by the State Coastal Conservancy, the Wildlife Conservation Board, and the Regional Water Quality Control Board; another 25% came from regional government agencies including the County of San Luis Obispo and the City of Pismo Beach; and the last 10% poured in from excited donors who recognized the Preserve as a stunning recreation resource, a vital protection for the land and wildlife, and a boon for nearby businesses.

After several years of thoughtful planning, LCSLO, with the help of the Wallace Group and other local businesses, partnered with Precision Construction Services of San Luis Obispo and R. Burke Corporation to create an entranceway, a parking lot, a main kiosk area with information and restrooms, and an array of solar panels to power the entire property. Most prominent, of course, were the 11 miles of world-class trails that offered an endless assortment of experiences, challenges, and route variations. Designed and built in collaboration with Central Coast Concerned Mountain Bikers (CCCMB, another local

*Ever since it opened, the Preserve has been the repeated winner of "Best Hike" awards, like the one proclaimed on this 2024 banner posted in the main kiosk area.*

# THE HISTORY OF THE PISMO PRESERVE

non-profit organization), the network of interlacing trails could be enjoyed by hikers with all different skill levels, interests, and schedules; by casual and serious mountain bikers; by horseback riders, runners, families, naturalists, solitude seekers, dog owners, residents, tourists, photographers, poets … in short, by virtually everyone.

Following ribbon-cutting ceremonies highlighted by speeches from local leaders, state officials, and representatives of ytt Tribe, the Pismo Preserve officially opened on January 25, 2020.

*Besides offering natural beauty, the Preserve provides scientific information to UC Berkeley. On Radio Tower Road near marker I15-2 is a seismic monitoring observatory. Part of the ShakeAlert earthquake early warning system, this active station sends data to the school's seismology lab.*

The public enthusiastically embraced this beautiful new treasure and swooped in to indulge in its sublime joys. In fact, the Preserve has been so well-received that it has blown past even the most optimistic projections for attendance: early predictions estimated 100 visitors a day, but in reality, daily attendance has consistently achieved four and five times that number all year long.

While this heavier-than-expected use is welcome, it's also taxing. More visitors mean more stress on the land and the animals, more trail maintenance, more restroom cleaning, more supplies, and more staff.

In addition, programs run by LCSLO, such as docent-led hikes and educational Learning Among the Oaks field trips for kids, have proven to be very popular. All of this maintenance, and all of these programs, depend on volunteers and donors. Learn how you can help at lcslo.org.

Throughout its history, the Pismo Preserve has been established and maintained in close collaboration with ytt Tribe, whose ancestors lived here and who still consider this land to be sacred. The creation of the Pismo Preserve was completed with sensitivity and respect, not just for the benefit of the environment and wildlife, but for its cultural significance. As was proclaimed during the opening-day ceremonies, the glorious Pismo Preserve epitomizes the theme of "doing things right the first time."

## LOCATION AND OPERATIONS

*On a hot July afternoon, downtown Pismo Beach, just a mile away, sparkles in the sun. This view, looking southwest from the east side of the Preserve, is from the upper Discovery trail; a lower section of Discovery slices across and around the hill to the right.*

*There's no highway sign announcing the Pismo Preserve, so along Highway 101 look for Exit 191B to Mattie Road. This northbound view shows the Preserve's hills beckoning in the background.*

### LOCATION

With its convenient location in the heart of the Central Coast, the Pismo Preserve offers an easily accessible recreational opportunity for residents and vacationers alike. In fact, the Preserve is so conspicuous along this stretch of coastline that it is clearly visible from the main highway and from all around the area.

The Preserve's entrance is just minutes from popular landmarks. Dinosaur Caves Park and Shell Beach are a half-mile to the north; downtown Pismo Beach and the Pismo Pier are a mile to the south; the Oceano Dunes are three miles to the south. On the other side of the Preserve's coastal mountains, downtown San Luis Obispo is about a dozen miles away. Anyone driving north or south on Highway 101 through Pismo Beach will see the Preserve on the east side of the highway (directly opposite on the highway's west side is a prominent row of popular coastal hotels). Exit 191B will get you to the southern end of Mattie Road. A 100-yard ascent towards the hills leads to the Pismo Preserve's entrance at 80 Mattie Road.

## LOCATION AND OPERATIONS

### PARKING

The ADA-compliant parking lot has 54 parking spaces: 47 for cars and trucks, four for motorcycles, and three for vehicles with disability placards.

*At left, the empty parking lot on a damp March morning, and at right the busy parking lot during a July special event.*

In addition, three large spaces with movable cones are designated for horse trailers only; these spots must be reserved in advance (lcslo.org/PismoHorseParking or 805-544-9096). Equestrians are reminded to please pack out your horse's manure from the parking lot and leave the ground clean. Rakes and other helpful tools are provided near the horse trailer parking zone.

In general, the Preserve's parking lot is busiest on weekends, holidays, and in mid-morning hours. Should the parking lot be full, additional free parking is available within walking distance along Price Street on the west side of Highway 101.

### HOURS

The hours of operation are easy to remember. The Preserve is open 365 days a year, even on holidays, from dawn to dusk. However, that dusk closing is firm: the parking lot gates are locked after sunset, and any vehicle not out of the lot by then will stay overnight until the following dawn.

Generally, the Preserve's only unscheduled closures are due to rain. To protect the trails, the entire Preserve is closed during and after rain events; some trails may remain closed longer following significant storm events. Typically, these closures only occur in the winter and early spring, but they can last for a week or more. Check for closures by consulting "Trail Status" at lcslo.org/pismo-preserve/.

# Rules

*Stay on trails*

*Pack it out*

*No smoking*

*No camping*

*No fires or grills*

*No collection of resources*

*No harassment of wildlife*

Visitors are expected to know and follow the basic rules that keep the Pismo Preserve safe and ensure a pleasurable experience for all.

The Preserve is an environmentally sensitive area that could easily be destroyed by carelessness. The land is especially vulnerable to fire. For most of the year, the dry, grassy hills are highly flammable, so several important rules are intended to minimize the threat of fire.

Smoking is strictly forbidden everywhere and at all times on the property. In addition, no campfires or grills are allowed anywhere.

Because the Preserve is designed for "passive recreation" (human-powered or horse-powered), pedaled bikes are permitted, but e-bikes and other motorized vehicles are not.

Additional rules are designed to safeguard the wildlife and their fragile habitats. No camping is allowed anywhere; no flowers, plants, or other resources are to be taken; no weapons and no drones are permitted. At the Preserve, wildlife is always around you and is always to be protected.

To keep the Preserve experience as pure and natural as possible for all visitors, no amplified sound is allowed on the trails.

Dogs are allowed but must always be on a leash (for their own safety as much as for anyone else's); also be sure to bring one of the plastic waste bags that are available in the parking lot.

*No motor vehicles*

*No e-bikes*

*Use bike bells*

*No weapons*

*No drones*

*No amplified sound*

*Dogs on leash*

# Rules

Be mindful of staying on designated trails and paths, and always pack out any trash you generate (there are no trash cans or waste receptacles beyond the immediate parking lot area).

By following all of these rules and guidelines, you are helping to keep the Pismo Preserve a beautiful natural sanctuary that can be enjoyed by everyone.

*Starting in November 2024, the popular Vamonos trail was closed for almost four months after a fire ravaged the surrounding hills.*

## ANIMALS AND BIRDS...

Though an abundance of wild animals call the Preserve home, many of them only come out once all of the visitors have left. At night, cameras mounted throughout the property regularly capture images of such prominent residents as bobcats, bears, and mountain lions, plus coyotes and deer. Smaller inhabitants include skunks, weasels, wood rats, voles, various lizards, king snakes, rattlesnakes, and Pacific tree frogs.

In addition, over 80 bird species, from hawks and falcons to turkeys and quail, make their homes in the Preserve, though many are heard more than they're seen. Butterflies often flit around the flora, especially in the migratory winter months.

Eye-to-eye with a western fence lizard, the harmless reptile often seen on the trails, on the fire roads, and in the parking lot.

A surprise encounter with a turkey vulture on the Lone Oak trail in late July.

Visitors didn't even have to leave their cars to observe this handsome red-tailed hawk perched on a fencepost in the parking lot one July afternoon.

Crows cluster in the fields, soar over the trees, and hang out near the entrance.

A king snake alongside High Road in July. Photo by CJ Silas.

A West Coast lady butterfly near Vamonos in August.

A swallowtail butterfly up on Radio Tower Road in June.

## ...AT THE PISMO PRESERVE

Red-winged blackbirds are among the Preserve's most commonly seen residents. Photo by Kaila Dettman.

Two rattlesnakes beside the Discovery trail in August. Photo by Wyatt Stapp.

A deer high up on the Preserve at 2 a.m. on June 15, 2019.

A bear coming down a fire road at 7 p.m. on October 4, 2023.

A California whipsnake (aka striped racer) coiled in the parking lot in October.

A bobcat walking a trail at 3 a.m. on November 4, 2023. All night-camera photos are courtesy of LCSLO.

A mountain lion prowls a trail at 9 p.m. on September 30, 2023.

## A BOUQUET OF FLOWERS...

Horticulturists, botanists, home gardeners, and flower lovers will find plenty to admire at the Pismo Preserve, especially in the spring and early summer (everyone is invited to look, of course, but no one is allowed to collect any of the flora or fauna). The following photos, all taken while standing on the trails, identify just a few of the Preserve's colorful blooms. Except for the Black Mustard, Milk Thistle, and Pot Marigold, these are all native plants.

*Black Mustard*  *Bush Lupine*  *Bush Monkey Flower*

*California Orange Poppy*  *California Yellow Poppy*  *Coast Morning Glory*

*Coast Paintbrush*  *Fiesta Flower*  *Figwort*

## ...AT THE PISMO PRESERVE

*Hummingbird Sage*

*Lacy Phacelia*

*Milk Thistle*

*Pismo Clarkia*

*Pot Marigold*

*Western Vervain*

*A field of poppies and other wildflowers on a spring morning. Photo by Kaila Dettman.*

## Exploring the Trails
# Pismo Preserve Trail Map

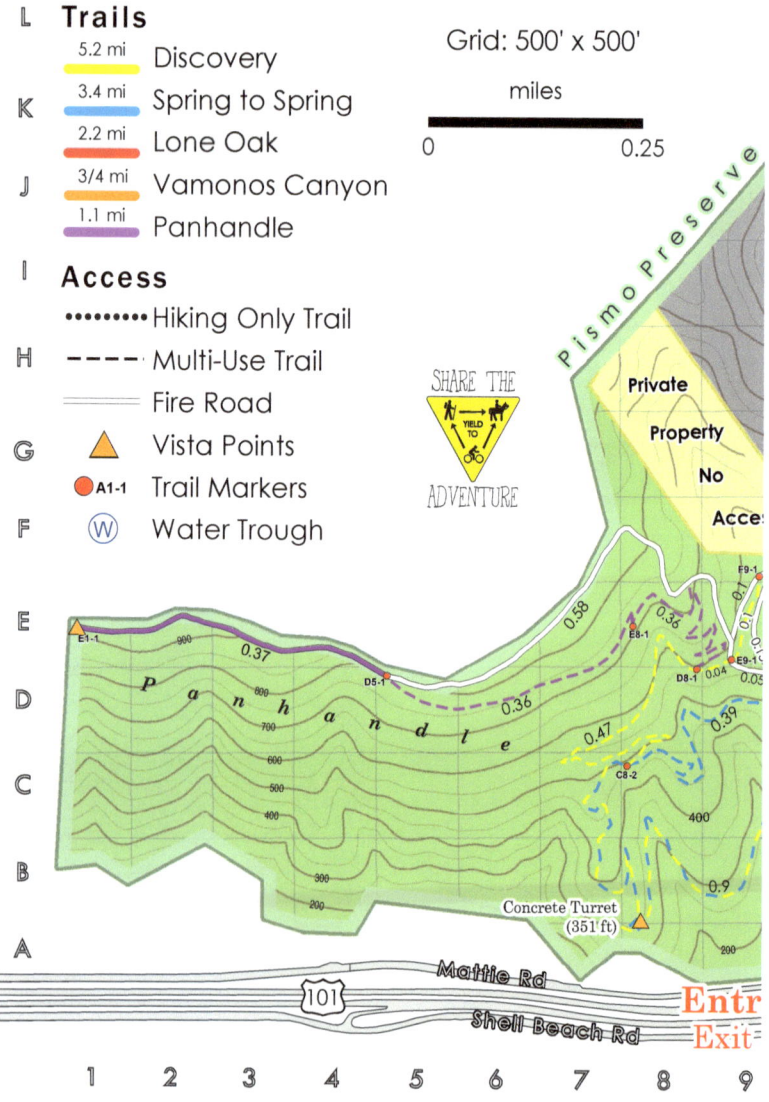

# EXPLORING THE TRAILS

## The Four Fire Roads

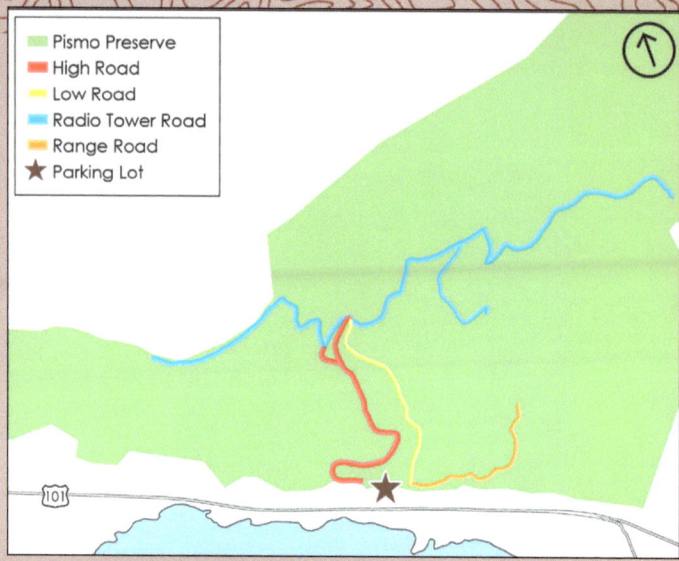

### High Road
Length = .61 miles (approx. 1,600 paces*)
Lowest point = 200' | Highest point = 550'
Difficulty = Hard

### Range Road
Length of the main trail = .45 miles (approx. 1,100 paces)
Lowest point = 200' | Highest point = 350'
Difficulty = Moderate

### Low Road
Length = .46 miles (approx. 1,300 paces)
Lowest point = 200' | Highest point = 550'
Difficulty = Hard

### Radio Tower Road
Length = 1.78 miles (approx. 4,600 paces)
Lowest point = 550' | Highest point = 850'
Difficulty = Moderate

*Throughout this detailed discussion of the Preserve's trails and fire roads, we occasionally use "paces" as a general measurement. This rough approximation equals about 30 inches and is intended as a helpful way to gauge distances. The number of paces we give is the rounded-off number of paces we really counted as we walked that stretch. Obviously, everyone's stride is unique, downhill paces may be different from uphill or flat paces, and energetic start-of-the-hike paces may contrast with tired end-of-the-hike paces, so your actual mileage may vary.

*Most of High Road is in full sun, but short sections provide welcome shade and enticing westward glimpses of the blue ocean just beyond.*

*Low Road starts its climb northward towards the top of the Pismo Preserve.*

## EXPLORING THE TRAILS: FIRE ROADS

### TRAIL TALK

Every discussion of the Preserve's five main trails includes at least one mention of the four fire roads lacing through the property. Wide enough for emergency vehicles, these unpaved, rough roads provide access and shortcuts that savvy visitors can use to their advantage. As an added bonus, the views from the roads are usually sublime.

Three of the roads are quickly reached from the parking lot. At the west end, High Road begins its sunny ascent to marker B10-1 and veers to the right where the Discovery and Spring to Spring trails veer to the left. High Road then rapidly climbs 300 feet in just over half a mile, finally topping out at marker F9-1 some 550 feet above sea level. Wildflowers line much of this trek in the spring and summer.

Halfway to F9-1, the Knoll, a flat meadow on your left, is a scenic highlight offering four picnic tables and panoramic views from 430 feet above sea level. A little farther up High Road, the Spring to Spring trail intersects at marker D10-1 for some west-east hiking options.

From the parking lot's east end, Low Road is a major route rising straight up the Preserve's spine towards a northern rendezvous with Radio Tower Road. Like High Road, Low Road rises 300 feet, but Low Road makes this climb in a shorter distance, so vertically it's a more challenging route. Two main trails–Vamonos, some 700 paces up at marker D11-2; and Spring to Spring, another 400 paces beyond at E9-2–cross Low Road to offer perpendicular paths of varying lengths. Nice shaded sections along Low Road mitigate the full sun.

*The low-elevation Range Road provides close views of the imposing rocks that divide Highway 101 as it runs through Pismo Beach. Left behind as erosion claimed the rest of the hills, these rocks are called an ancient sea stack. Looking south, downtown Pismo and the Pismo Pier are in the distance.*

Also leaving from the parking lot's east end is Range Road, which hugs the coast and rises only 200 feet above its starting point. Three main trails bump into Range Road. Discovery, Lone Oak, and Spring to Spring all begin (or end) at A13-1 close to the parking lot, and all three touch Range Road again farther up.

## EXPLORING THE TRAILS: FIRE ROADS

*The eastern half of Radio Tower Road makes a steady ascent up to some of the Preserve's highest elevations ...*

*... and continues on right past the Notch, a short offshoot that presents scenic glimpses but no further access beyond this point.*

The northern end of Range Road runs into the Lone Oak trail at C14-1. Because Range Road is always near the noisy highway passing below, it doesn't offer much seclusion, but it is a handy downhill shortcut back to the parking lot after long hikes on the main trails.

Running west-east across the top of the Preserve is Radio Tower Road. Unlike High Road, Low Road, and Range Road, Radio Tower Road is not directly accessible from the parking lot. What's more, it's both the longest (more than the other three roads combined) and the highest (800+ feet) of the four fire roads.

The biggest challenge involving Radio Tower Road is simply reaching it. The Discovery trail offers a long, winding upward walk that meets Radio Tower Road at several points, while the shortest routes are via High Road and Low Road, which climb up through the

## Exploring the Trails: Fire Roads

middle of the Preserve to meet the midpoint of Radio Tower Road.

From this "Grand Central Station" intersection where the three roads meet near marker F9-1, 1800 westward paces on Radio Tower Road take you past glorious ocean views and several rest stops. The walk bends west and east as it steadily climbs before flattening out for the final quarter-mile to D5-1. There the Panhandle trail takes over for the last leg out to the scenic Avila Overlook.

Instead of heading west from F9-1, another option is to head east for 2800 paces to reach Radio Tower Road's end point. The mile-long trek starts with long, relatively flat sections that lead to H12-1 and the Notch, a 694-foot-high vista point with narrow northeastern views but no trail access beyond its locked gate. A short southbound offshoot near the Notch leads to a large circular trough where equestrians can get water for their mounts.

From H12-1, bear southward to the right on Radio Tower Road for 100 paces to H13-1, and continue up for 100 paces to a picnic table. From this restful spot informally known as "the Perch," count 200 more paces up to an unmarked dirt path that aims right to the top of a hill. Radio Tower Road continues to the left, but this unmarked path to the right points to one of the Preserve's highlights. About 200 paces up this path is the Five Cities Overlook, an open summit with two picnic tables and a majestic 360-degree view. The 900-foot-plus elevation here rivals the highest point to the Preserve's far west, the Avila Overlook. A notebook permanently attached to one of the tables invites praising comments.

Return the 200 paces back to Radio Tower Road, and continue eastward (right) for 500 mostly downward paces to marker I15-2. Here the way is crossed by the scenic Peek-a-Boo Loop mini-trail (see page 33). Continue straight on Radio Tower Road for a quarter-mile of up-and-down hills to I17-1 and the road's end point (the tall radio tower this route is named after is clearly visible ahead of you but is inaccessible). You could return the way you came, but at I17-1 there's an option to take Peek-a-Boo Loop southward to I15-1, where the main Discovery trail connects for a long descent to the parking lot. As you make your way down these two miles, you'll see the nearby streets and houses of Pismo Heights to the east, but none of that neighborhood can be reached from the Preserve.

## DISCOVERY TRAIL

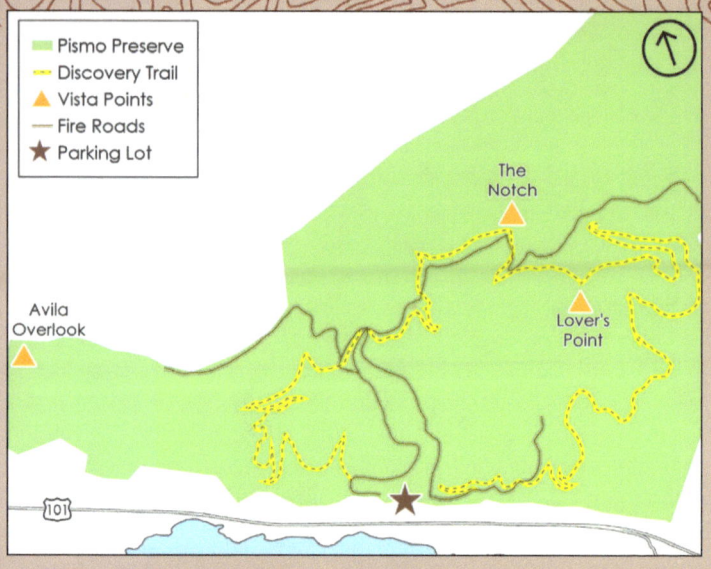

## TRAIL FACTS

Length of the main trail = 5.2 miles
(approx. 14,000 paces)
Lowest point = 200'
Highest point = 700'
Difficulty = Easy to Moderate

*The Discovery trail often wraps back upon itself as it winds across the hills, as seen here in late April.*

## TRAIL TALK

The full grandeur of the Pismo Preserve is gloriously revealed on the Discovery trail. By far the Preserve's longest hike, Discovery winds around the hills for 5.2 miles (almost two miles more than the next-longest trail, Spring to Spring). Discovery circles the Preserve's wide perimeter and presents scenic views of the hills, ocean, and coastal towns. While the trail is rarely steep or difficult, the sheer length of the walk presents a challenge, especially as hiking time edges past three hours to four.

Begin your hike at the western edge of the parking lot and head up to the big map posted at marker B10-1. Fork to the left for half a mile (about 1300 paces) in the full sun to reach the Concrete Turret. This map landmark may disappoint visitors who expect to see an impressive military or scientific installation but instead find a three-

## EXPLORING THE TRAILS: DISCOVERY

foot-tall, six-foot-wide concrete block half-buried in the weeds. At one time it likely served as the base for military survey equipment for the guns operated by the 54th Coast Artillery during World War II on the bluffs of Shell Beach. The 54th Coast Artillery was the first Central Coast Black Combat Unit to be placed into operation in our county.

Continue through rolling switchbacks for another 1000 paces to marker C8-2. While you're still close enough to civilization to hear faint highway sounds, you've also been making a gradual ascent up to 500 feet above sea level and are now about 30 minutes from the parking lot.

Here at C8-2, Discovery bears upwards to the left, Spring to Spring down to the right. Continue up Discovery in and out of

*Here it is, the glorious Concrete Turret in all of its splendor. This "landmark" is halfway between markers B10-1 and C8-2 along the Discovery trail.*

trees for another 1400 paces (and another 100 feet in elevation) to marker D8-1, where a small map is posted. Take a moment to indulge in views of beauty and the beach: those are Pismo, Grover, and Oceano beaches curling to the south. Continue a quick 60 paces across the wide High Road to E9-1, and then another 300 paces on Discovery take you to F9-1 and the major intersection (nicknamed "the Octopus") where Discovery, High Road, Low Road, and Radio Tower Road all converge.

Now an hour into your hike, you've got several options for a return to the parking lot if you're ready to head back. From F9-1 go 50 paces to F9-2 and turn right towards the ocean for a steep half-mile descent on Low Road. If you stay on Discovery, another 600 paces take you to F11-1, where the Connector mini-trail (see page 33) leads to Spring to Spring and a different route down to the parking lot.

With half of Discovery behind you and another half ahead, intrepid hikers can take

## EXPLORING THE TRAILS: DISCOVERY

*As seen in mid-May from the Preserve's verdant west side, the views from high up on Discovery take in the Knoll (the open field with picnic tables in the center), plus downtown Pismo Beach and the Pismo Pier.*

a left at marker F11-1 to continue Discovery's steady upward climb for another 350 paces. Cross the dirt fire road at G11-1, go straight for another 800 paces to H12-1 (the Notch, 694 feet above sea level), and continue upwards a short distance to H13-1. Stay on the rocky, narrow, uphill trail to reach a picnic table.

Another 500 paces take you to an important intersection at G14-1. Here you can veer right for a quick diversion on the Lover's Point mini-trail (see page 33). Or, go left at G14-1 for 1600 paces to I15-1, which opens to views of San Luis Obispo and offers a detour on the Peek-a-Boo Loop mini-trail (see page 33).

To stay on Discovery, at marker I15-1 head downhill for two-thirds of a mile through intermittent trees to F16-1. A small map here reminds you that Discovery is now wrapping around the Preserve's eastern-most hills.

### TRAIL TIP
A complete walk on Discovery takes about 14,000 steps and around three hours. If you add the east-side detours to Lover's Point (600 paces and .16 miles roundtrip) and the Peek-a-Boo Loop (2400 paces, .8 miles), you'll walk a total of about 17,000 paces for almost four hours, and you'll see some of the Preserve's grandest vistas.

A right at F16-1 takes you up to the Lone Oak trail, and a left continues your Discovery hike down towards the coast. Descend some 700 paces through trees, past a south-facing bench, and to a cattle gate. From here amble across open plateaus with a long, gentle slope to a majestic rock and a fork to Lone Oak at C15-1.

Continue on Discovery for 1300 paces towards the highway and B14-1, and it's all downhill from here on the short jaunt to the parking lot.

## LONE OAK TRAIL

### TRAIL FACTS
Length of the main trail = 2.2 miles
(approx. 8,800 paces)
Lowest point = 200'
Highest point = 500'
Difficulty = Easy to Moderate

*Gently descending from trail marker D13-1, these are the last steps to the Lone Oak tree, as seen on a warm July afternoon.*

### TRAIL TALK

Not as sprawling as Discovery, as precipitous as Panhandle, or as frequented as Vamonos, Lone Oak offers a nice blend of moderate distance (just over two miles), easy ascents, long flat sections, and wonderful southern and eastern views. This less-traveled route is not to be missed.

Lone Oak begins and ends at marker A13-1, some 300 paces up from the gate at the east end of the parking lot. Take a left at A13-1 and make a steady ascent 200 paces up to A12-1. Aim right for 500 paces on an easy path that is shared with the Discovery trail, the Spring to Spring trail, and traffic noises from nearby Highway 101.

## EXPLORING THE TRAILS: LONE OAK

At B14-1, Discovery splits to the right, but you'll continue left 30 paces up Range Road to B14-2 and a sharp left. From here, Lone Oak and Spring to Spring overlap for an easy half-mile to B13-1. The mild ascent opens to westward views of the 1,200-foot-long Pismo Pier, surfers, and coastal hotels.

At marker B13-1, you'll begin a clockwise route directly to the tree the Lone Oak trail is named after. You'll pass a cattle gate, a west-facing bench, and a picnic table before getting a close-up look at the actual landmark.

At first it may be slightly underwhelming. Rising from rocks, the solitary oak reaches about 25-feet high and leans to one side. If it weren't isolated, the Lone Oak tree wouldn't seem much different from the thousands of other oaks sprinkled throughout the Preserve.

However, this is a tree with character. Its isolation confers the stately dignity of survival; furthermore, its very exceptionality makes this particular oak a familiar feature instantly recognizable from other trails and vantage points. To respect the tree's age (estimated at up to 200 years), and to discourage climbers, a rope blocks access.

*Near the Lone Oak tree, a view to the northwest shows High Road climbing on the far green hill from the center left to the upper right, and Vamonos descending down the nearer brown hill from the center to the lower right.*

Surprisingly, despite the 420-foot height of the hill, the most dramatic sightseeing isn't towards the ocean, it's towards the interior canyons and steep hills. A sweeping northern view brings in three of the Preserve's main trails and two fire roads, all of them snaking across the hills and passing through stands of trees while the tallest peaks in the background soar towards 1000 feet. Glorious.

Now about 30 minutes from the parking lot, make an easy ascent away from the ocean and up the trail for 300 paces to marker D13-1 and the start of a leisurely clockwise circle that will bring you back in sight of the Lone Oak tree. From D13-1, amble 1100 paces on the flat, open trail to F16-1, passing through two cattle gates and taking in

# Exploring the Trails: Lone Oak

*On the east side of the Preserve at C15-1, this ten-foot-tall natural rock formation marks the junction of the Lone Oak and Discovery trails.*

spectacular views of Pismo Beach, Arroyo Grande, and the dark, symmetrical volcanic core (919-foot Picacho) six miles to the east. F16-1 marks one of the highest points on Lone Oak, about 500 feet above sea level.

The easy stroll from F16-1 to C15-1 is, at .61 miles and 1800 paces, the longest stretch between two markers on the Lone Oak trail. Overlapping with Discovery, this section makes a gradual descent, passes a cattle gate and a bench, and ends at an imposing rock formation (shown above) that looks like it fell from the sky and landed next to the trail.

Continue westward from C15-1 for two minutes to reach C14-1. Cross over north-south Range Road and continue parallel to the coast for 300 flat paces to B13-1, which should look familiar. This is a marker you came to over an hour ago, the one that aimed you directly up to the Lone Oak tree.

### Trail Tip
A nice feature of the Lone Oak trail is its overlap with two other main trails, Spring to Spring and Discovery, for about a mile each. These overlaps mean that you can easily extend your Lone Oak hike in different directions simply by veering away to one of these other main trails. You also have options for rapid returns to the parking lot if you want to cut your Lone Oak hike short. As you curve westward from marker F16-1 in the homestretch, at C14-1 you can blast down Range Road for a half-mile to the parking lot instead of staying on Lone Oak for double that length.

Return to the parking lot by walking a gentle downhill slope for a half-mile to B14-2, and continue downhill for 30 more paces back to B14-1. Here you can either go back the way you came by winding westward to A12-1 and down to the parking lot; alternatively, you can shave off a few minutes and a tenth of a mile via the more direct Range Road (as usual, a fire road is the fastest route to the parking lot).

## PANHANDLE TRAIL

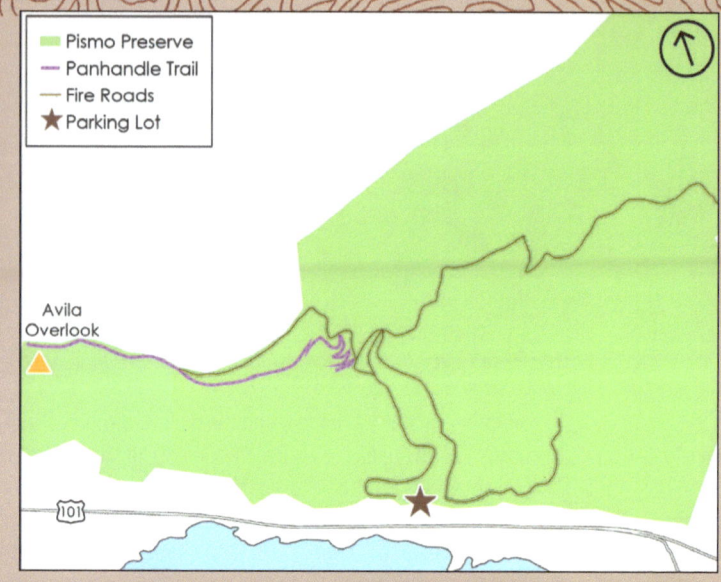

### TRAIL FACTS
Length of the main trail = 1.09 miles
(approx. 2800 paces)
Lowest point = 600'
Highest point = 950'
Difficulty = Hard (to reach the main trail), Moderate (on the main trail)

*Switchbacks and shade are abundant along Panhandle's first third of a mile as it climbs away from Discovery.*

### TRAIL TALK
Bring lots of exultant adjectives with you when you visit Panhandle. The views from these heights are among the most spectacular in the entire Preserve.

You'll have to earn those views, however. The uppermost section of Panhandle sprawls west-east along the highest ridge in these hills. It's getting to the ridge that's the challenge. You have to climb almost 600 vertical feet from the parking lot before you reach Panhandle's relatively flat western half.

## EXPLORING THE TRAILS: PANHANDLE

Spring to Spring and Discovery, two main trails detailed elsewhere in our pages, both get you to Panhandle's doorstep with winding mile-and-a-half routes that offer their own scenic pleasures. Both trails begin near the west end of the parking lot at marker B10-1, and both curl westward along the same hilly path for the first mile. Then, at C8-2, Spring to Spring and Discovery diverge. Spring to Spring continues eastward to meet the rising High Road at D10-1, while Discovery bears left and upwards for a half-mile to a rendezvous with the Panhandle trailhead at D8-1.

Once you're on Panhandle, the first third of a mile is notable for its many switchbacks. Resist the temptation to create your own shortcuts; instead, stay on the zigzagging trail and enjoy the remarkable southern views that take in distant mountains, Point Sal jutting into the ocean, and the far horizon. Canopies of shading oaks through here provide intermittent breaks from the direct sun.

*The view to the west from the Avila Overlook, looking down from over 900 feet above the ocean. The bright green area near the center on the other side of Highway 101 is Dinosaur Caves Park, while the town of Shell Beach spreads to the right.*

About 2000 paces and some 40 minutes from the parking lot you reach marker E8-1. The next third of a mile on Panhandle lopes easily along the high ridge extending westward (it's this stretch that gives the trail its name). D5-1 and a picnic table mark the last leg to the Preserve's western-most point.

Keep heading parallel with the ocean for another third of a mile to the Avila Overlook, Panhandle's terminus. Here the trail loops around two picnic tables and comes back, but this spot is worth a pause to stroll around and enjoy the scenery. From this skyscraping elevation you can see over the ridge to the northeast and to San Luis Obispo. Avila Beach is visible to the north, Shell Beach's Dinosaur Caves Park sprawls to the west. Relish the dizzying view of Highway 101 directly below—you're looking down from a towering summit that's as high above the sea as if you were atop the Eiffel Tower.

## EXPLORING THE TRAILS: PANHANDLE

If there's extreme satisfaction in making it this far (and this far up), there's extreme pleasure in cruising comfortably to the parking lot, because Panhandle and High Road are almost all downhill. Everywhere you look, generous ocean and Preserve vistas beckon. The entire two-hour walk from the parking lot up High Road to Panhandle's Avila Overlook and back covers approximately 3.5 miles and requires almost 10,000 paces, many of them strenuous. But nobody ever says that the effort wasn't worth it.

*As seen on a clear July afternoon, the views to the north and northeast from the highest point on Panhandle are breathtaking.*

### TRAIL TIP
The shortest route from the parking lot to Panhandle is via the steep High Road. From the parking lot's west end, head up the wide path to marker B10-1 and take a right onto High Road (the sunny trek up High Road is detailed on page 15). Pass C11-1 and D10-1, and then take a left at the orange High Road Control Line sign. Continue northward 250 uphill paces to E9-1, where the Discovery trail crosses west-east. Go left on Discovery for a flat 100 paces to D8-1 and turn right to officially begin the three-foot-wide Panhandle trail.

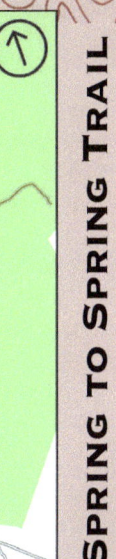

## SPRING TO SPRING TRAIL

**Map Legend:**
- Pismo Preserve
- Spring to Spring Trail
- Fire Roads
- Vista Point
- Parking Lot

### TRAIL FACTS
Length of the main trail = 3.4 miles (approx. 9000 paces)
Lowest point = 200'
Highest point = 520'
Difficulty = Moderate (to reach the main trail), Moderate (on the main trail)

*For most of Spring to Spring, the walk is easy, the views delightful.*

### TRAIL TALK
Spring to Spring resembles Discovery, but in two-thirds of the distance and with two-thirds of the elevation. Whereas Discovery wraps a wide loop around the Preserve's perimeter, Spring to Spring is like a concentric circle inside that loop. Both trails begin and end at the same places (B10-1 to the west, A13-1 to the east), both trails overlap for almost a mile, and both trails span the Preserve to offer exhilarating views of ocean and canyons.

Begin your trek at the west end of the parking lot and walk 200 paces up the open High Road to the big map. Spring to Spring (marked with a blue arrow) and Discovery

## EXPLORING THE TRAILS: SPRING TO SPRING

(yellow arrow) both begin with a left turn here at B10-1. Make a steady ascent on this broad trail through switchbacks for about 1300 paces to the Concrete Turret and a west-facing bench (the meager Turret is described in detail in the Discovery section).

Staying roughly parallel with the coastline and the highway below, continue upwards 1000 more paces past two separate west-facing benches to C8-2. At this marker where Spring to Spring and Discovery split up, you've now been walking for about a half-hour and covered almost a full mile.

The 1000 paces from C8-2 to D10-1 are some of the easiest in the entire Preserve. You're no longer hiking through here, you're sauntering. The wide, flat trail winds through shading trees, passes a restful bench, and presents a series of expansive views. Halfway along this section is one of the many springs intersecting this trail, though water runs only in the rainy months.

*With the Lone Oak tree at your back, look northward to see Spring to Spring heading upwards to the right and eventually coming across the hill to the left-center. Discovery is crossing the high distant hill in the center.*

As you cross the wide north-south High Road, you'll see the D10-1 marker that guides you eastward. Continue on the easy trail in the full sun for 300 paces to E9-2. The small spring here, which has a 40-foot-long low wooden walkway curving across it, is one of the two springs this trail was named after (the other is near F13-1 to the east).

From this marker to F11-2 a half-mile away, Discovery is running parallel about 100 feet above you to the north. This stretch of Spring to Spring crosses the steep north-south Low Road, passes atop a low, curving wooden bridge (another spring, usually dry, is underneath), visits a west-facing bench, and ends close to this main trail's highest point (over 500 feet above sea level). Approximately halfway through your Spring to Spring hike, you're now about an hour from the parking lot.

At F11-2, take a right heading down. The markers come quickly: 150 paces to F12-3, then 100 to F12-2, another 100 to F12-1, and 250 to F13-1. From here, great gnarled

## EXPLORING THE TRAILS: SPRING TO SPRING

oaks that look like they belong in an enchanted fairy-tale forest punctuate the shaded fifth-of-a-mile stroll to D13-1. After the first 75 of this section's 600 paces you'll cross another spring bed that's dry for most of the year. Waiting for you at D13-1 are wonderful 360-degree panoramic views that take in the entire Preserve and coast.

With the main Lone Oak trail heading off to the left, at D13-1 take a right for the effortless amble down 300 paces to the prominent Lone Oak tree (a landmark detailed in the Lone Oak section). As the trail wraps south around the tree, 300 paces will take you past a west-facing bench, through a cattle gate, and to marker B13-1.

At this point you're only about 20 minutes from the finish line. Take a sharp right at B13-1 and descend 1400 paces to B14-2. A fast 30 paces bring you down to B14-1, where you'll take a right to follow the blue arrow. This last short stretch of Spring to Spring begins with a gentle slope and ends at A12-1. After a 200-pace descent to A13-1, the parking lot is just two minutes away. Your two-hour Spring to Spring hike began at the parking lot's west end, looped around the Pismo Preserve's beautiful interior, and now culminates at the parking lot's east end.

*Halfway along Spring to Spring as you head towards the ocean, a rapid series of markers lowers you from F11-2 to F13-1 some 600 paces away. You'll notice that two of these markers, F12-2 and F12-1, offer two parallel paths, but the choices aren't really that varied, because they all basically get you to the same end points and cover generally the same short distances.*

*The only real difference is the obvious steep grade of the options, as shown in the top photo taken at marker F12-1. Explore the rising/falling uphill/downhill routes only if you feel like adding an extra challenge and an extra couple of minutes to your hike. The lower photo shows the crisscrossing options, with Spring to Spring entering from the far left at F12-2, and the aforementioned F12-1 standing where X marks the spot at the right.*

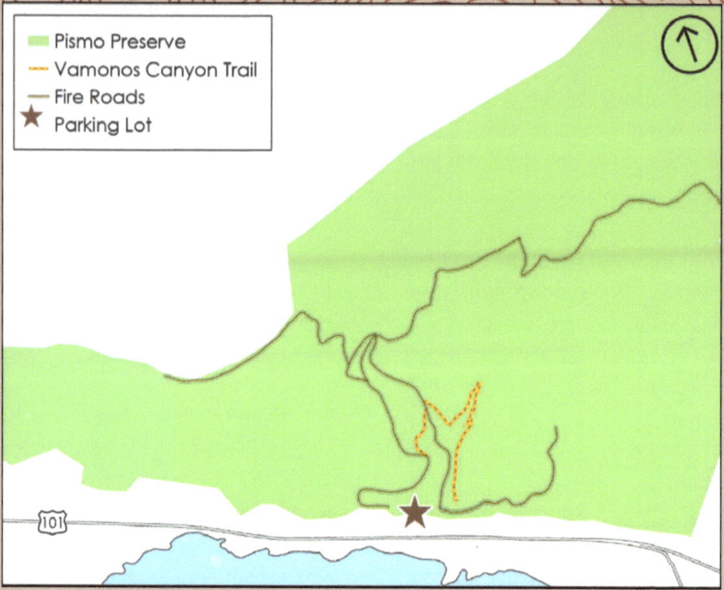

## VAMONOS TRAIL

### TRAIL FACTS
Length of the main trail = .76 miles
(approx. 2000 paces, no bikes or horses)
Lowest point = 200'
Highest point = 300'
Difficulty = Moderate (to reach the
main trail), Easy (on the main trail)

*Under a canopy of oaks, this rest stop along Vamonos overlooks the trail curling below and to the left.*

### TRAIL TALK
Looking for a short, scenic, relatively easy walk through shady trees? Vamonos is your trail. While other hikes are steep and sun-drenched, this one is level and sun-dappled.

Covering about three-fourths of a mile over mostly flat, single-file terrain, Vamonos (Spanish for "let's go") is accessed at either end by moderate uphill slopes.

From the east end of the parking lot, head down the paved path to the gate, bear

## EXPLORING THE TRAILS: VAMONOS

right up Range Road, and turn left at marker A13-1 in the direction of Lone Oak. The six rocky, uphill steps here may present a challenge for some hikers.

Continue another 200 paces through a switchback to A12-1. Here you formally begin the Vamonos trail with a northward walk that overlooks the parking lot, the ocean, and the Pismo Pier to the south. An illustrated sign near marker A12-1 posts "Vamonos Trail Notes" about the flora and fauna you're about to encounter.

Continue through a small gate and head away from the coast. As the narrow trail aims into the hills, the parking lot disappears from view, highway sounds recede, and bird songs amplify on the gently rolling path. Soon you're in full shade beneath a canopy of oak trees. In the winter and spring, a small creek flows to your left. Now some 15 minutes from the parking lot, you cross a small bridge under a fallen tree. A short ascent takes you to another small bridge, more switchbacks, and finally a shaded rest area with two benches. Watch for poison oak around this area all year long.

*From High Road and marker C11-1 on a May afternoon, Vamonos can be seen climbing from the lower left up to a scenic bench perched atop the rocks in the center.*

From the benches, continue along the trail and carefully ford the tiny creek nearby. Another 100 paces will leave the shade behind you and put you in full sun.

You're now heading towards the ocean again; a lone bench mounted atop a rock-strewn hill along this route affords an impressive view to the distant westward horizon. This bench (shown above) is the approximate halfway point of your Vamonos hike.

## EXPLORING THE TRAILS: VAMONOS

*This little bridge in the Vamonos woods leads hikers under a dramatic trail-hurdling tree. The creek below the bridge runs fast in the spring but dries out by August, when this photo was taken.*

By now you've walked about 1000 paces with almost 1000 ahead, but these will be mostly downhill. Continue 200 paces to a small bridge that leads to marker D11-2, where the wide Low Road crosses. Low Road's downward slant takes you towards the ocean and returns you to the parking lot.

You've now completed an easy loop that's taken you across Vamonos and back down via Low Road in about 30-40 minutes. Observant hikers will have taken in many eye-catching sights, but they probably haven't seen any bike riders, as they're not allowed on this long section of Vamonos between A12-1 and D11-2.

Near D11-2 is an easy extension to your pleasant half-mile Vamonos walk. Head down Low Road just 20 paces to D11-1 and bear right for a gentle westward continuation of Vamonos. Go 350 sunny paces to C11-1 and High Road, then take 800 downhill paces to the parking lot's west end.

### TRAIL TIP
Detailed above is the Vamonos-to-Low-Road route; the reverse hike frontloads the most strenuous section in the first 15 minutes. From the parking lot hike up Low Road, turn right at marker D11-2, and continue up to the lone scenic bench (shown in the photo on the previous page). You'll then cruise the next 1000 paces back to the parking lot with ease. Whether you start with Vamonos or with Low Road, you'll be greeted with plenty of ocean vistas and nature sounds.

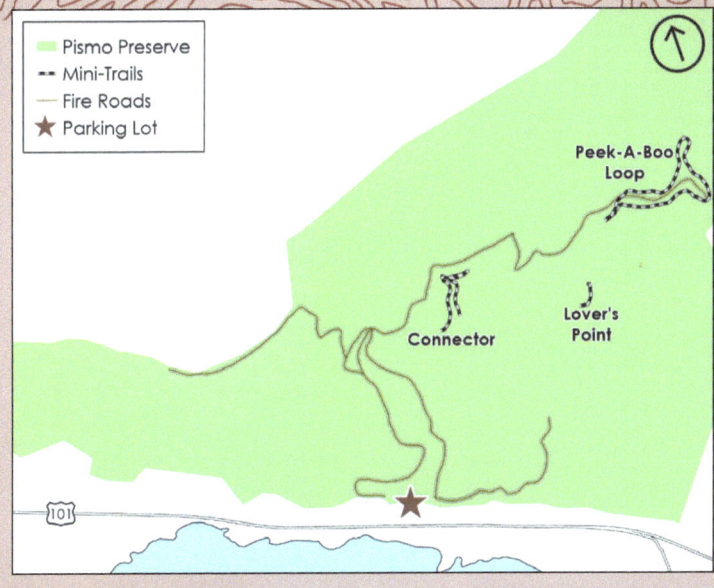

## THE THREE MINI-TRAILS

### TRAIL FACTS

**CONNECTOR**
Length = .37 miles
(approx. 1,000 paces)
Lowest point = 500'
Highest point = 600'
Difficulty = Easy

**LOVER'S POINT**
Length = .16 miles
(approx. 300 paces,
no bikes)
Lowest point = 750'
Highest point = 780'
Difficulty = Easy

**PEEK-A-BOO LOOP**
Length = .79 miles
(approx. 2,300 paces)
Lowest point = 650'
Highest point = 700'
Difficulty = Easy

*Looking northward along the Peek-a-Boo Loop mini-trail on an August afternoon.*

*An afternoon walk in July along the short Connector mini-trail.*

## EXPLORING THE TRAILS: MINI-TRAILS

*A panoramic view to the north from Lover's Point on a hot May afternoon.*

### TRAIL TALK

One of these short mini-trails is a handy link between two main trails; the other two mini-trails offer scenic side trips away from two main trails.

As its name suggests, Connector is a convenient shortcut between Discovery and Spring to Spring. Hikers who have ascended Discovery from the west end of the parking lot will have already walked 1.81 miles and climbed up about 500 feet, so a return to the parking lot might look attractive right about now, especially on a hot day.

In the heart of the Preserve, marker F11-1 offers that chance.

Here Discovery continues upwards to the left and wraps around the Preserve's eastern perimeter for another 3.4 miles; meanwhile, Connector peels off to the right and presents a gentle downward-sloping alternative. Go 1000 paces on this easy trail and enjoy the intermittent shade and the ocean vistas.

The last section of Connector near F11-2 reveals Spring to Spring running parallel below and to the left. At F11-2 continue straight on Spring to Spring for a half-mile towards the ocean (a south-facing bench offers a scenic respite midway through your trek). After hiking ten minutes on Spring to Spring, you reach Low Road and its precipitous slope to the parking lot.

Deep into the Discovery trail, having walked over an hour from either the west or the east, you have the option at marker G14-1 to veer onto another mini-trail, this one a memorable detour to Lover's Point. You'll appreciate the romantic name once you zigzag 300 paces (about two minutes) to an isolated south-facing bench. From this lofty perch 780 feet above sea level, the extraordinary views might be punctuated by wide-winged hawks lazily circling below you. The only way back is via the way you

## Exploring the Trails: Mini-Trails

came, making this total walk about a sixth of a mile. Note that no bikes are allowed along this mini-trail.

The next mini-trail, Peek-a-Boo Loop, is actually longer than the main Vamonos trail, but it's still considered an offshoot of the Discovery trail. To get the namesake view on Peek-a-Boo Loop, climb steadily upward on Discovery for over an hour (about three miles from the parking lot if you're coming from the west, two from the east) to reach I15-1. From I15-1, the looping roundtrip on Peek-a-Boo Loop back to this marker will take about 2300 paces, the first half moderately uphill. At I15-1, go 200 paces to I15-2 and continue 1300 paces past a south-facing bench to I17-1. From there a final 800 paces return you to I15-1 and the re-connect with Discovery. At its summit, Peek-a-Boo Loop reaches 700 feet above sea level and presents distant views to the north, including San Luis Obispo's agricultural lands and the Santa Lucia mountain range 15 miles away.

*A northeast view on an August morning from Peek-a-Boo Loop, with Price Canyon Road winding northeast in the left-center, a line of dark train tracks in the right-center, and the distant Santa Lucia range in the background.*

## TRAIL SUPERLATIVES

The following assessments are based on a mix of geographical facts and subjective opinions compiled after spending hundreds of hours on the Pismo Preserve's 11 miles of trails and fire roads.

**SHORTEST OF THE FIVE MAIN TRAILS**

- Vamonos, .76 miles (30-40 minutes)

**LONGEST OF THE FIVE MAIN TRAILS**

- Discovery, 5.2 miles (three-four hours)

**BIGGEST ELEVATION GAIN OF THE FIVE MAIN TRAILS**

- Discovery, over 500'

**TWO HIGH-ELEVATION PICNIC TABLES IN THE PRESERVE**

- Panhandle, 916' at marker E1-1 (see photo below)
- Unmarked path and hill east of H13-1, approx. 800'

**STEEPEST WALKABLE SECTION OF THE PISMO PRESERVE**

- Low Road from E9-2 to F9-2, .08 miles to climb 100'
  (a slope averaging 24%, at times it may feel almost double that)

**THREE MAIN TRAILS WITH LONG RELATIVELY FLAT SECTIONS**

- Spring to Spring, 1.36 miles from C8-2 to D13-1
- Discovery, .61 miles from F16-1 to C14-1
- Lone Oak, .41 miles from D13-1 to F16-1

*The highest picnic table at the western end of Panhandle on a July afternoon.*

*Welcome shade along the Spring to Spring trail in early June.*

## TRAIL SUPERLATIVES

### THREE MAIN TRAILS WITH LONG SHADED SECTIONS

- Spring to Spring, .39 miles from C8-2 to D10-1 (see photo on previous page)
- Panhandle, .36 miles from D8-1 to E8-1
- Vamonos, .25 miles in the center section between A12-1 and D11-2

### TWO MAIN TRAILS WITH PANORAMIC VIEWS OF THE SOUTHERN COASTLINE

- Discovery from G14-1 to F16-1
- Lone Oak from D13-1 to F16-1

### TWO MAIN TRAILS WITH PANORAMIC VIEWS OF THE NORTHERN COASTLINE

- Discovery from C8-2 to D8-1
- Panhandle from D5-1 to E1-1 (the Avila Overlook)

### TWO WEST-FACING BENCHES WITH PANORAMIC VIEWS OF THE OCEAN

- East side: Lover's Point, 780'
- West side: Discovery trail, 350 paces up from the Concrete Turret (halfway between the Concrete Turret and C8-2)

### A MAIN TRAIL, MINI-TRAIL, AND FIRE ROAD WITH PANORAMIC VIEWS OF SAN LUIS OBISPO AND NORTHERN MOUNTAINS

- Panhandle from D5-1 to E1-1
- Peek-a-Boo Loop from I15-2 to I17-1
- Radio Tower Road from H12-1 to I15-2

### GREATEST DISTANCE FROM HIGHWAY 101 AND ITS SOUNDS

- Upper end of Peek-a-Boo Loop, approx. 1.25 miles

*At left, Lover's Point on an August afternoon. At right, a late-afternoon view in May from a west-facing bench on Discovery. Views towards Shell Beach from the benches on Discovery are technically from Spring to Spring too, since these two main trails overlap for almost a mile on the Preserve's western side.*

## SEASONAL VARIATIONS

Regular visitors to the Pismo Preserve are familiar with the conspicuous month-to-month changes in the landscape. Rainfall, which is heaviest in January and February (averaging three inches per month) and lightest in July and August (averaging *zero* inches per month), has the greatest effect on the Preserve's flora.

In the spring, when light rains can sometimes sprinkle into late May, fresh wildflowers bloom brightly across the hills and tall grasses ripple in shades of green. A photographer's dream, the Preserve feels alive with running streams, brilliant colors, and new life during these vernal months.

*Above, a view of the Discovery trail as it passes between green hills in May. Below, just a month later Discovery is now cutting across brown hills, with most of the spring grasses and flowers just a memory.*

## Seasonal Variations

In contrast, the hot, dry summer months, when temperatures rise into the 90s, desiccate those same streams, and turn the parched hills brown. While the trails are dusty from the summer into the fall, the sunny sky blazes clear and blue, making the magnificent ocean views sharper and stronger than ever. The dazzling scenery will bring out the poet in you.

Even if the weather conditions are colder and wetter in the winter and early spring, these months do offer a terrific scenic advantage: migrating gray whales. From December to February the grays, the most commonly sighted whales, are southbound to their Mexican calving lagoons, and then from February to April they're northbound to their Alaskan feeding grounds. Less-seen humpback whales and even rarer blue whales are on the move from May through August.

Any of these whales might be glimpsed spouting or even breaching in the waters just off Pismo Beach. Naturally, whale sightings aren't guaranteed from the Pismo Preserve, but they are numerous and always memorable.

Special events are infrequent at the Preserve, so as to keep the parking lot and trails wide open for all visitors. One special event especially popular with kids is the annual mid-July celebration of World Snake Day. Held under tents at the Knoll, a grassy meadow up High Road about 700 paces from the west end of the parking lot, World Snake Day presents a chance to see all variety of live snakes, including rattlers. Adventurous visitors are allowed to touch and even handle some of the benign specimens.

*An invited guest (not a Preserve resident), this six-foot-long boa constrictor dropped in to visit World Snake Day.*

# Recommendations and Etiquette

## Enjoying the Trails

For your own safety and enjoyment, be sure to take advantage of the restrooms in the main kiosk area before starting your hike, as there are no other facilities anywhere in the Preserve. Take water with you, because there are no water fountains beyond those in the parking lot area.

*Early in November, morning mist cools the main kiosk area in the parking lot.*

Prepare for full sun and extreme heat from late spring to late fall. Hats, sun screen, sunglasses, and other protections are essential. Note that there are no artificial structures–such as sheds, overhangs, canopies, etc.–anywhere on the trails that provide shade.

Before heading out, be sure to plan your hike or bike ride at the big map in the parking lot (or at marker B10-1 just north of the parking lot); once you get up into the hills, there are only four small maps posted along the 11 miles of intertwining trails. A detailed trail map is available at lcslo.org/pismotrailmap.

• • • • • • • • • • • • • • • • • • • • • • • • • • • • • • • • • • • • • • • • • • • • • • • • •

Exploring the Preserve on a bike is one of the most efficient ways to appreciate the entire property. Responsible mountain bike riding is welcome on all of the Preserve's trails except in two places: on the short Vamonos trail between markers A12-1 (near the east end of the parking lot) and D11-2 (a half-mile into the canyon); and on the spur that starts at G14-1 and extends to Lover's Point. For the rest of the Preserve's trails, the gentle grade is ideal for both uphill climbing and downhill riding.

One of the most popular routes among mountain bikers is riding the Discovery trail counterclockwise, a 5.2-mile loop that begins with a gentle climb and ends with an enjoyable downhill through oak woodlands back to the parking lot. Riders looking to tack on some more mileage can take a quick detour through the Peek-a-Boo Loop or up to the Panhandle for panoramic views.

E-bikes are not allowed on any of the Preserve's trails. Cyclists are required to use

## RECOMMENDATIONS AND ETIQUETTE

a bell to ensure safety for both riders and other trail users. Bells can be borrowed at the bottom of Range Road (A13-1) and High Road (B10-1), but please be sure to return your bell when you complete your ride. Riders are required to always ride responsibly and in-control when exploring the Preserve.–Christa Stoll, Community Engagement Coordinator, LCSLO. Photo by LCSLO.

### TRAIL ETIQUETTE

Since nearly all of the Preserve's 11 miles of trails are shared equally among hikers, bike riders, and horseback riders, there are some basic etiquette guidelines to ensure that everyone derives equal enjoyment. As many posted signs remind everyone along the trails, bike riders yield to both hikers and equestrians; hikers yield to equestrians; equestrians always have the right of way.

Because the Preserve's trails and fire roads are unpaved, rocky, and often steep, they may be challenging for some visitors, especially those on crutches or those who use manual or powered wheelchairs. The Land Conservancy has partnered with Positive Ride to provide the use of Freedom Trax to enable expanded access for everyone. These free battery-operated attachments and chairs are available to anyone with mobility issues but must be reserved in advance. Learn more at positiveride.com or by emailing positiveride1@gmail.com.

*Travis Jecker, founder of Positive Ride, explores Low Road using Freedom Trax. Photo by Kaila Dettman.*

Scattered throughout the Preserve, often in the most scenic locations, are well over a dozen picnic tables and individual benches. Do avail yourself of any of these, but please refrain from marking them in any way.

As always, be watchful and courteous on the trails. Blind single-file corners, like the section shown on the next page that banks around a sharp curve on Discovery, could easily have runners, bike riders, or equestrians rapidly approaching from the opposite direction with little warning.

# Recommendations and Etiquette

### Trail Safety
While the trails are generally well-maintained and safe, they are still passing through wilderness areas where natural hazards exist. There are also many tight switchbacks and narrow corners, like the one shown at left on Discovery, where sudden encounters with oncoming visitors are possible. Always be alert and remember that safety is paramount.

Wildlife is always abundant at the Pismo Preserve, even when you can't see it around you. All wildlife at the Preserve is to be respected and given the right of way. Furthermore, close-up encounters with wildlife must be avoided, for both their safety and yours. Wildlife can behave unpredictably, and even carry rabies, so never reach for a live wild animal or touch a dead one. Always stay on the trails and fire roads, and dog owners must keep their pet on a leash so it won't stray into the brush.

Some plants at the Preserve are also hazardous. Poison oak flourishes in these hills, especially in the spring and summer, so be careful where you reach, step, or sit. Additionally, everyone who brushes up against any tree, plant, stump, or pile of leaves is possibly exposing themselves to ticks.

*Taken in December, this aerial photo looks northward to "the Octopus," an upper level of the Preserve at trail markers F9-1 and F9-2. Radio Tower Road drops from the upper-left and stretches across to the center-right edge. Just below it on the left side is the squiggly Discovery trail that reaches towards the green field in the center and then drops below Radio Tower Road on the right side. Descending from the bright green field are two wide fire roads, High Road (angling to the lower-left corner) and Low Road (coming almost straight down); both routes plunge to the parking lot a half-mile away. Photo by Christa Stoll.*

## RECOMMENDATIONS AND ETIQUETTE

Anyone seriously injured at the Pismo Preserve should call 911. If possible, identify your location by the nearest trail marker (E8-1, F11-2, etc.) so that first responders can find you. If you are on a trail and want to get to your car as quickly as possible, access the nearest fire road (High Road, Range Road, etc.), as it will provide the speediest route down to the parking lot.

The Pismo Preserve welcomes equestrians and offers several amenities to make your horseback ride convenient and enjoyable. Note that it's BYOH (Bring Your Own Horse) at the Preserve, as The Land Conservancy does not offer its own horseback riding excursions.

Because the Preserve's trails are often narrow and are visited by hundreds of hikers and mountain bikers each day, The Land Conservancy advises against bringing inexperienced horses or riders to the trails. In addition, equestrians are advised to carry the same bike bells that are required for mountain bikers, and all riders are urged to wear helmets.

Horseback riders will encounter several livestock gates throughout the property. For horse and rider safety, it is recommended to dismount and walk your horse through the gates when they are closed. Mounting blocks are located at each gate for your convenience. Please leave all gates as you found them.

Please do NOT tie horses to trees along the trails. Tie rails are provided on the Preserve's west side at the Avila Overlook and on the east side near map marker H13-1 (see this map on pages 12-13). These spots also have picnic tables and make for great locations for both horse and rider to rest while taking in the amazing views. Note that a large water trough is located high up in the center of the Preserve between map markers F12-3 and H12-1, but there are no troughs in the northwestern sections of the Preserve or along the Panhandle trail, so plan accordingly.

Several local equestrian groups participated in the fundraising, design and ongoing maintenance of the equestrian amenities at the Preserve, including Backcountry Horsemen of California (Los Padres Unit); Ride Nipomo Equestrian Trails Alliance; the Atascadero Horsemen's Association; and San Luis Obispo Parks Open Space and Trails.–Kaila Dettman. Photo by LCSLO.

## ABOUT THE LAND CONSERVANCY

**TOGETHER WE SAVE SPECIAL PLACES**

The Land Conservancy is a local non-profit 501(c)3 accredited land trust that serves San Luis Obispo County. Its mission is to conserve and care for the diverse wildlands, farms, and ranches of the Central Coast, and to connect people to the land and to each other.

The organization has a large variety of projects and programs. LCSLO is perhaps most well-known for restoring the Octagon Barn in San Luis Obispo and opening it as a community gathering space, and for the Pismo Preserve, a beloved nature preserve opened in 2020 and visited by 200,000 people per year.

Since its founding in 1984, LCSLO has protected over 67,000 acres of land through conservation easements and outright purchase, and it has restored sensitive habitats in local streams and coastal dunes ecosystems. The Learning Among the Oaks nature education program is embedded in our local public

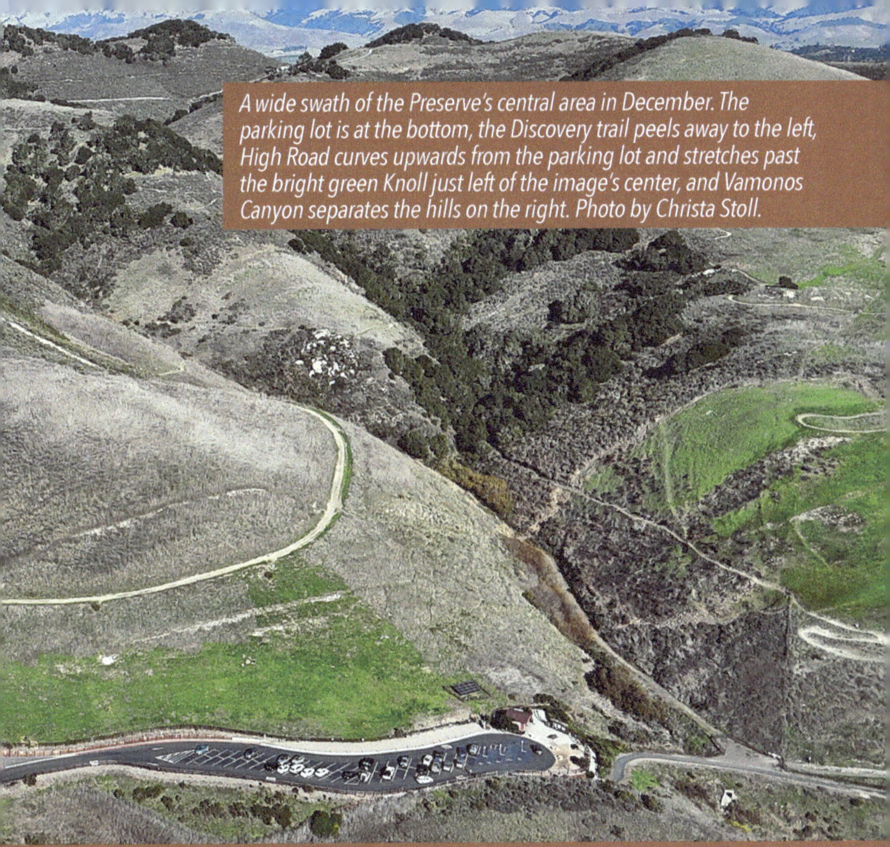

*A wide swath of the Preserve's central area in December. The parking lot is at the bottom, the Discovery trail peels away to the left, High Road curves upwards from the parking lot and stretches past the bright green Knoll just left of the image's center, and Vamonos Canyon separates the hills on the right. Photo by Christa Stoll.*

schools and focuses on kids to teach them about the wonders of nature through place-based learning at nearby trails. LCSLO also hosts docent-led hikes and activities on conserved land throughout the County—connecting people with nature for their own well-being and to cultivate a love of our local lands and wildlife.

LCSLO is funded through local, state, and federal grants, and donations from generous supporters. The organization has an extremely dedicated staff and volunteer board, plus amazing volunteers who help with everything from trail maintenance to fundraising.

Website: lcslo.org • Phone: (805) 544-9096
Email: info@lcslo.org • Fax: (805) 544-5122
Office Address: 1137 Pacific St, Suite A, San Luis Obispo, CA 93401
Mailing Address: PO Box 12206, San Luis Obispo, CA 93406

### ABOUT THE AUTHOR

This is Chris Strodder's sixteenth book. Much of his work has explored and celebrated popular culture, from Disneyland© history to classic movies. A longtime Pismo Beach resident, Chris can often be found at the Pismo Preserve serving as an official volunteer.

Email: pismopreservers@gmail.com

*Meandering across the Preserve's highest hills, Radio Tower Road eventually climbs to the summit seen in the center of this July photo. Standing over 900 feet tall, this eastern hill is topped by the spectacular viewpoint known as the Five Cities Overlook.*

## "GOT LOST BUT FOUND THIS GEM!"

*More of the messages written in the "legacy notebook" stationed atop the Five Cities Overlook along Radio Tower Road (as described on page ii).*

"Be creative, curious, and kind. Life is so much more interesting when you are inquisitive. Work your hardest and don't settle (but make time for memories, that's wayyy more important). You have so much to be grateful for."

"Believe in simplicity."

"I just want to say that I hope everyone reading this learns how to fly in this life, how to truly enjoy every moment. Most never do because in order to fly you must jump, and that's a scary thing to do. Jumping into something that is unfamiliar, uncomfortable, and scary is never easy, but neither is dying knowing you never tried."

"Drove by this mountain all my life—just look!! Think of the things we drive by every day and of the amazing things we can do."

"Beautiful view of Lover's Point, ocean, and mountains, with a cool breeze and birds chirping and flowers growing. Glorious!"

"How beautiful is this place God created for us long before we came here. Hallelujah."

"El dia de padre, y yo aqui apaciando este dia" (Father's Day, and I am here enjoying this day).

"As with everything in life, effort is rewarded, and here the long walk up the trails to reach this steep hilltop has brought a beautiful celebration of perfect nature."

"Life is too short to be angry and sad, be grateful and take a moment to be present."

"Be kind, be positive, and live life, as none of us is getting out alive."

"Expand your horizons—ride in the opposite direction."

"From the top of the highest mountain, the view is so beautiful that I don't want to leave. I'm so excited to see this beautiful view!"

"Beyond beautiful! Thank you Land Conservancy!"

## PISMO PRESERVE CHECKLIST

How many of these places have you explored?

**MAIN TRAILS**
- ☐ Discovery
- ☐ Lone Oak
- ☐ Panhandle
- ☐ Spring to Spring
- ☐ Vamonos

**MINI-TRAILS**
- ☐ Connector
- ☐ Lover's Point
- ☐ Peek-a-Boo Loop

**FIRE ROADS**
- ☐ High Road
- ☐ Low Road
- ☐ Radio Tower Road
- ☐ Range Road

**VISTA POINTS**
- ☐ Avila Overlook
- ☐ Concrete Turret
- ☐ The Knoll
- ☐ The Lone Oak Tree
- ☐ Lover's Point
- ☐ The Notch

FAVORITE TRAIL:

FAVORITE BENCH/VIEW SPOT:

FAVORITE TIME OF DAY AT THE PRESERVE:

FAVORITE MONTH/SEASON AT THE PRESERVE:

ANIMAL AND BIRD SIGHTINGS:

*These two aerials were taken in December, 2024 from the same spot, but they point in opposite directions. The top photo aims northward with the Preserve's hills on the right, Highway 101 in the middle, Shell Beach on the left, and Avila Beach in the distance. The bottom photo takes a southward look at the Preserve on the left, with the parking lot, Highway 101, and Pismo Beach all on the right. Photos by Christa Stoll.*

# FIELD NOTES

www.ingramcontent.com/pod-product-compliance
Lightning Source LLC
Chambersburg PA
CBHW040935030426
42337CB00006B/57